BUSINESS SELLING INSIGHTS
VOL. 4

BUSINESS SELLING INSIGHTS

VOL. 4

SPOTLIGHTS ON LEADING BUSINESS INTERMEDIARIES, BROKERS, AND M&A ADVISORS

FEATURING LEADING BUSINESS INTERMEDIARIES, BROKERS, AND M&A ADVISORS

Jimmy Royall
Jason Pittman
Barbara Kline
Bob Dunphy
Lauren Drummond-Dale
Kevin A. Nery
Kelly M. Hayes
Virginia Altman
"JT" Jim Tatem
Michael D. Mauger

Copyright © 2022 Remarkable Press™

All rights reserved. No part of this publication may be reproduced, distributed, or transmitted in any form or by any means, including photocopying, recording, or other electronic or mechanical methods, without the prior written, dated, and signed permission of the authors and publisher, except as provided by the United States of America copyright law.

The information presented in this book represents the views of the author as of the date of publication. The author reserves the right to alter and update their opinions based on new conditions. This book is for informational purposes only.

The author and the publisher do not accept any responsibilities for any liabilities resulting from the use of this information. While every attempt has been made to verify the information provided here, the author and the publisher cannot assume any responsibility for errors, inaccuracies, or omissions. Any similarities with people or facts are unintentional.

Business Selling Insights Vol. 4/ Mark Imperial —1st ed.
Managing Editor/ Shannon Buritz

ISBN: 978-1-954757-21-9

Remarkable Press™

Royalties from the retail sales of **"BUSINESS SELLING INSIGHTS Vol 4: SPOTLIGHTS ON LEADING BUSINESS INTERMEDIARIES, BROKERS, AND M&A ADVISORS"** are donated to the Global Autism Project:

AUTISM KNOWS NO BORDERS; FORTUNATELY NEITHER DO WE.®

The Global Autism Project 501(C)3 is a nonprofit organization that provides training to local individuals in evidence-based practice for individuals with autism.

The Global Autism Project believes that every child has the ability to learn, and their potential should not be limited by geographical bounds.

The Global Autism Project seeks to eliminate the disparity in service provision seen around the world by providing high-quality training to individuals providing services in their local community. This training is made sustainable through regular training trips and contiguous remote training.

You can learn more about the Global Autism Project and make direct donations by visiting **GlobalAutismProject.org.**

CONTENTS

A Note to the Reader ix

Introduction xi

Jimmy Royall 1

Jason Pittman 11

Barbara Kline 23

Bob Dunphy 35

Lauren Drummond-Dale 49

Kevin A. Nery 61

Kelly M. Hayes 71

Virginia Altman 81

"JT" Jim Tatem 93

Michael D. Mauger 107

About the Publisher 115

A NOTE TO THE READER

Thank you for obtaining your copy of "BUSINESS SELLING INSIGHTS Vol. 4: Spotlights on Leading Business Intermediaries, Brokers, and M&A Advisors." This book was originally created as a series of live interviews on my business podcast; that's why it reads like a series of conversations, rather than a traditional book that talks at you.

My team and I have personally invited these professionals to share their knowledge because they have demonstrated that they are true advocates for the success of their clients and have shown their great ability to educate the public on the topic of buying and selling businesses.

I wanted you to feel as though the participants and I are talking with you, much like a close friend or relative, and felt that creating the material this way would make it easier for you to grasp the topics and put them to use quickly, rather than wading through hundreds of pages.

So relax, grab a pen and paper, take notes, and get ready to learn some fascinating insights from our Leading Business Intermediaries, Brokers, and M&A Advisors.

Warmest regards,

Mark Imperial
Publisher, Author, and Radio Personality

INTRODUCTION

"BUSINESS SELLING INSIGHTS Vol. 4: Spotlights on Leading Business Intermediaries, Brokers, and M&A Advisors" is a collaborative book series featuring leading professionals from across the country.

Remarkable Press™ would like to extend a heartfelt thank you to all participants who took the time to submit their chapter and offer their support in becoming ambassadors for this project.

100% of the royalties from this book's retail sales will be donated to the Global Autism Project. Should you want to make a direct donation, visit their website at GlobalAutismProject.org

JIMMY ROYALL

JIMMY ROYALL

CONVERSATION WITH JIMMY ROYALL

■ **Jimmy, you are the founder of Tri East Commercial in North Carolina. Tell us about your work and the people you help.**

Jimmy Royall: We're a commercial real estate and business brokerage firm just east of Raleigh, North Carolina. We are located in a fast-growing area, and many people are moving here and starting businesses. So it's an excellent opportunity. I'm a native here. I grew up here and studied at the University of North Carolina. So I've got a lot of contacts. We help people sell their properties, purchase properties, sell their businesses, and purchase businesses here in this fast-growing area outside of the Research Triangle in Raleigh, North Carolina.

LEADING BUSINESS INTERMEDIARIES, BROKERS, AND M&A ADVISORS

> ■ **What concerns do clients have when they reach out to you for the first time?**

Jimmy Royall: Many owners selling their businesses may have thought their children would take over, but their children have decided to do something different and aren't interested. Also, the interest in the area is driving prices up. There is a great transfer of wealth going from one generation to another. So that makes it opportunistic for people to sell their businesses at a good price. We deal with many smaller businesses between $1 million and $5 million. Often, they are not big enough to employ a merger acquisition firm or investment banking firm. So they need good advice. They may have a lawyer and an accountant, but they really don't understand how to market a business. So we go in and work with their professionals to evaluate the business and develop a marketing plan and then put it out there to our nationwide network. I'm a part of EXP Commercial, a fast-growing real estate company. We started a commercial division last year, and many people are joining in. So we have a lot of contacts around the country, and people are looking to move into this area because it's a great area to operate a business.

> ■ **How has the "Great Resignation" impacted your market?**

Jimmy Royall: Many people want to own businesses due to the pandemic and other issues. They need to work with a company like mine to help them evaluate opportunities, ensure they are getting a good value, and understand what they are buying. Often, with small businesses, your income stream and your payments are tied up in the owners. It is important to be able to separate that and really understand the earning potential of the business when deciding to acquire.

■ Are there myths and misconceptions about selling a business?

Jimmy Royall: People really have no idea what their businesses are worth. They tend to think in terms of hard assets. They don't know how to evaluate cash flow, return on investment, and other factors that play into the valuation of a business. So in a confidential way, we help owners figure out what they're doing. In most cases, they don't want their employees or family members to know they are thinking about selling. We always operate with confidentiality and help them determine what their business is worth, how the process works, and what to expect.

■ What common mistakes do sellers make?

Jimmy Royall: The biggest mistake is not separating their operating income from personal expenses. We try to help owners understand the difference so that when people come in to buy, they see they've got enough money to pay for the financing of that business to give them a good return on their investment and pay themselves a fair salary or return on investment. Many people who run small businesses have their personal checking accounts mixed in, so we help them sort it all out.

■ How far in advance should an owner prepare for the sale of their business?

Jimmy Royall: It can be a drawn-out process; it's not like selling a house or a piece of real estate. Many times, it's an emotional sale. People have built the business from scratch, becoming like their child. It's hard for them to let it go. So there is a process of talking to the family and the spouse, then evaluating and coming up with a fair price and a price they will accept and enjoy.

In addition, many buyers moving from corporate life to buying a business need some help to get started. Often, our sales are structured so that the owner stays on for a year or two and gradually moves out of the business to ensure success. It helps the new buyers understand it, work with it, and learn about the customers. So the entire process can actually take a couple of years.

■ Jimmy, what inspired you to get started in this field?

Jimmy Royall: After I graduated from school, I spent a couple of years in the banking industry and then started my own business.

I've owned several businesses and bought several businesses, and I enjoy it; I understand it. Unlike real estate, where there are plenty of real estate agents, there are few business brokers out there, and people don't use them that often. But it can really save people a lot of money and make people a lot of money. I think we are a very valuable part of the process. So since I have a lot of experience and I know many people in the area who trust me, it's just a matter of getting out there and helping them. And it's fun to do. I'm not really looking to buy businesses for myself anymore. I'm looking to help others enjoy that, especially younger people who want to get into a business and see it grow.

■ Is there anything else you would like to share?

Jimmy Royall: Do your proper research, especially if you are not working with someone like myself who has the experience and can help you find a business, evaluate your business, market your business, and help you get the most for your investment and your life work. Whether you are a buyer or a seller, working with us improves your chances of getting a better deal.

LEADING BUSINESS INTERMEDIARIES, BROKERS, AND M&A ADVISORS

■ **How can people find you, connect with you, and learn more?**

Jimmy Royall: My website is www.trieastnc.com. You can also email me at jroyall@trieastnc.com. We are in Johnston County, North Carolina, just east of Raleigh.

JIMMY ROYALL

Founder

Tri East Commercial

WEBSITE:
www.trieastnc.com

EMAIL:
jroyall@trieastnc.com

JASON PITTMAN

JASON PITTMAN

CONVERSATION WITH JASON PITTMAN

■ **Jason, you are a business broker with Exit Advisor LLC in Chicago, Illinois. Tell us about your work and the people you help.**

Jason Pittman: I work with owner-operated small businesses, typically under $10 to $20 million in revenue in the Chicago Metro. These owners are thinking about selling their business or starting to think about exit planning. They have questions like, "What do I need to work on now to get the business more sellable? How do I increase the value and form an exit strategy?"

■ **How informed are sellers when they first reach out to you?**

Jason Pittman: I'd say it's a pretty mixed bag. Some of them are prepared, and they've been thinking about it as part of their business planning. And some of them have even started their business with the exit in mind. Then some folks really just started their businesses as a side hustle. Or perhaps it was a way of just owning a job. But then it grew and grew and became a business. So I think some people are ready for the exit. Some people have great businesses and don't even realize they could sell them.

> ■ How has the "Great Resignation" impacted the Chicago market?

Jason Pittman: It has brought more buyers into the market because many people are looking for their first business to acquire and are willing to relocate. So I feel there's more of that than even a few years ago. We have the "Silver Tsunami" and the "Great Resignation" playing out in this area. Some people have just decided that now is the time to retire. Some are having banner years and are choosing to sell while everything is going up, while others have quite the opposite story. So everything that is happening right now has made significant changes in the industry.

> ■ How far in advance should an owner prepare for the sale of their business?

Jason Pittman: I would say you should always be preparing, and you should always be thinking about an exit strategy. Many business owners who came to us were not planning on selling. Something unexpected happened, whether death, a health issue, or burnout, forcing them to sell. Whatever the case may be, you should think about the concept of having a sellable business so you can have a safer asset in the event something unexpected happens. It would help if you worked on having clean financials and not running a lot of personal expenses through the books. You need to substantiate expenses down to the penny to a buyer and their lender team. It would be best to think about excess inventory and equipment you don't really need to have around. Are there any key suppliers or employees that you are very reliant on? Would they be hard to replace? And then, most importantly, how reliant on you is the business? Do you own a job? Or do you own a business? It will be harder to sell your business if you own a job and are right in the middle of everything.

- **Are there myths and misconceptions about selling a business?**

Jason Pittman: There is a big misconception about how easy it is to sell a business. It's not easy at all. People have it in their heads that it's more of a commodity like real estate. If you have a house or an income-producing property like a four flat or a six flat, that is more a commodity than a business. So it's more about just finding the right price to get it sold. On the other hand, a great business that turns profits has so many more moving pieces that can make it unsellable. That's the big difference. Business owners just think, "Well, I've got this number in my mind, and I just need to go list it like a house, and then I'm done." That is the biggest misconception.

■ What mistakes do sellers make?

Jason Pittman: A big mistake is not reporting all of their income. Sometimes it is very tempting to have a side source of income from a wholesale customer, and they choose not to report that income. Well, now they're complicating things. The same goes for running personal expenses through the business that would be hard to substantiate, like personal vehicles and vacation homes. It's better to leave those things off while you are leading up to selling. As business owners, working with an accountant to determine what legitimate expenses and deductions can be taken to minimize taxable income is a perk. But when you're in the mode of getting your business ready to sell, you should be thinking a little bit differently. You should be showing as much profit as possible and increasing the value, making things really simple and clear for a buyer, almost like if you were staging a house.

■ Jason, what inspired you to become a business intermediary?

Jason Pittman: My first career was working for Allstate in Northbrook's data center. Somewhere around year four or five, I got bit by the entrepreneurial bug. I knew I wanted to do something in real estate or small business. I wanted to work on my own, but I didn't know exactly what. Somebody gave me the idea of looking at buying an existing business. So I started looking for a business to buy on my own. And back then, I was in my mid-20s. So I was looking at pizza places and hand car washes. Ultimately, I didn't find anything that was a good fit for me. But I ended up hitting it off really well with one of the brokers I contacted on his listing. It was entirely coincidental. They were looking for someone they could train, and that's how I got into the business back in 2005.

■ Is there anything else you would like to share?

Jason Pittman: One of the things I'm trying to get people to think more about is the concept of salability. I think we ought to be thinking more about what makes a business sellable versus the number we're going to assign to the value. And I think we get too hung up on that number. Questions about what makes the business sellable are good questions to ask in terms of raising awareness and getting owners to think about the right things.

■ **How can people find you, connect with you, and learn more?**

Jason Pittman: I'm pretty easy to find on LinkedIn. My company is Exit Advisor LLC. Our website is www.exitadvisor.org, which will put you in touch with our team and current listings.

JASON PITTMAN

Business Broker

Exit Advisor LLC

Business owners work with Jason to sell their business or to increase the value and "sellability" of their companies in preparation for their exit.

Jason's unique focus is on educating and advising his clients to *prepare* their businesses for an eventual sale, whether they want to sell or not.

LEADING BUSINESS INTERMEDIARIES, BROKERS, AND M&A ADVISORS

Why? Because the same qualities that make a business really sellable are the same qualities that make owning a business fun and profitable, not to mention simple to transition to family or employees. It also makes the business a safer asset to have if life happens to throw you any sudden curveballs.

When the time comes to exit, Jason helps owners sell or transition their companies confidentially, often without the general public ever knowing.

Jason's areas of focus are Chicago area manufacturing and industrial businesses with annual revenues between $300k - $10M. But since he started in 2005, Jason has advised or represented a wide variety of traditional Main Street businesses and niche lower middle-market companies, from speed-dating to medical cannabis to defense suppliers. No matter what industry a business happens to be in, Jason has valuable experiences to draw on when helping clients with their exit strategy.

When Jason isn't working, he's spending time with his wife and three children, traveling, gardening, or taking on DIY projects around the house.

EMAIL:

jason@exit-advisor.com

PHONE:

800-551-2577

WEBSITE:

www.exit-advisor.com

LINKEDIN:

www.linkedin.com/in/jasonleepittman

BARBARA KLINE

BARBARA KLINE

CONVERSATION WITH BARBARA KLINE

■ **Barbara, you are a business broker with Absolute Investment Realty in Albuquerque, New Mexico. Tell us about your work and the people you help.**

Barbara Kline: A business broker assists in putting together people who want to sell a business and people who want to buy a business. A major part of that is the upfront work because running a business and selling a business require different sets of skills. I help business owners understand what they need to do to put a package together that somebody will buy. The target market for me is Main Street which is considered under $5 million in sales per year. It runs the full gamut of industries. Many of the folks I work with are in construction, service businesses, the food and beverage industry, and hospitality. It's delightful work; I really enjoy putting together win/win deals.

LEADING BUSINESS INTERMEDIARIES, BROKERS, AND M&A ADVISORS

▪ What are the biggest concerns people have when selling a business?

Barbara Kline: My personal website addresses many of those concerns (www.barbara-kline.com). Business owners don't always understand the reasons why someone wants to buy a business. Buyers look for an operating, successful business to reduce the risk of owning a Main Street business. Note that different dynamics are at play in many larger deals.

When an owner is selling a business, they must first show that the buyer will have enough money to live on. Secondly, they need to show that the buyer will have enough money to pay for minor expansions that may be necessary to grow the business. Nobody buys a business to be static – they have a vision and will need some money to start making the changes they want to implement; they expect that money to be generated from cash flow. Last, the typical buyer expects to recoup the purchase price within five to seven years fully. Sellers are competing with other investment vehicles and other businesses, and the expected returns those vehicles can provide the buyer. Buyer expectations can make a big difference in what a buyer is willing to pay and what a seller thinks something is worth.

My job is to make sure that the seller has the business packaged to make it viable for the buyer. It's an interesting dynamic. A lot of sellers pride themselves on *being* the business. That can be great, but what do you have to sell? I caution sellers not to have a story like, "Hey, we are fantastic! *I* do the sales; *I* do the design; *I* have the relationships." In that scenario, there is nothing for the buyer to buy. Also, sellers may see their business as a job replacement. This isn't a bad thing; it can be absolutely fantastic. But suppose you are running your business in a way that simply allows you to replace your salary (sometimes called a "lifestyle business") and have not added employees, procedures, and management that make it capable of operating without you. In that case, it is much harder to sell. Also, a business has to make money. This may seem obvious, but many tax advisors will support the concept that the closer you can get to zero in terms of what you're paying taxes on over the years, the better. It isn't easy to unwind that strategy when you're going to sell the business and want to demonstrate how much money the business can generate. It's also not easy to convince a bank to give your buyer a loan! I encourage people to start planning for selling at least three years before they actually want the event to happen. They need to have financial data in place to make it attractive and quick for someone to buy.

■ **How has the "Great Resignation" impacted your market?**

Barbara Kline: I have seen more sellers impacted by the "Great Resignation" than buyers, which I find interesting. The people participating in the "Great Resignation" are often moving from blue-collar work or work closely interacting with the public to a job that can be done more remotely. Those people often look for extra training or education to move to another employee position. On the other hand, owners have had some tough times over the last few years, and one of the significant issues has been the lack of availability of motivated employees. Many of the owners I talk to are really worn out and just want to move on. Many buyers I work with already have businesses and see this time as an opportunity to build and consolidate. In other words, if you're in construction, such as remodeling or window replacement, and you see a complementary company for sale, the odds are you won't need to have as many employees to run the two businesses together. I'm seeing people taking advantage of business opportunities to expand and do more with fewer employees; as the employees come back, these buyers will have an opportunity to leverage their combined companies for even greater growth.

■ **Barbara, what inspired you to get started in this field?**

Barbara Kline: I love to tell this story! I have a good friend and mentor who told me six years ago that I would be great in commercial real estate. He invited me to join the small firm he was with and introduced me to his partner. I had been doing marketing and business consulting in tech firms and startups for about 30 years, so this was a bit of a stretch. However, I have always had an interest in real estate and have invested in properties for quite a few years. I thought it would be fascinating. I studied for and passed the real estate licensing exam and got ready to work. Another door opened, and I studied for and received a Certified Business Broker designation. In the last five years, I have had a great time, I'm good at what I do, and I get excellent responses from the people I work with. For me, the experience I've had in other fields dovetails into what I'm doing now. I feel as if I've been preparing my whole life for this work, and I am ever so grateful to my mentor for his vision and belief in me.

> ■ **What should people look for when choosing a business broker?**

Barbara Kline: The most important thing is to find a broker with whom you resonate – someone you can trust. Selling (or buying) a business is a very collaborative program. It's not being a surgeon who can walk into an operating room, do a procedure expertly, and then leave the room and let the patient recover under the care of the referring doctor. My sellers and I have to be working together as a team, building upon each other's knowledge and resources to effect the best possible deal with the best possible buyer. If sellers are not comfortable with the business broker they're working with, it will be difficult to engineer a successful close. A potential seller also wants to look for a responsive business broker. This may not seem like that important of an issue, but when you're working on getting your business sold, it's nice to know that you have somebody who will call you back in a timely manner and keep you informed during the various stages of the sales process. I get a lot of feedback that this isn't always the case. Make sure you take the time to vet your broker upfront and feel comfortable with their interaction style.

LEADING BUSINESS INTERMEDIARIES, BROKERS, AND M&A ADVISORS

> ■ **How can people find you, connect with you, and learn more?**

Barbara Kline: You can reach me at barbara@go-absolute.net or barbara@barbara-kline.com. My phone number is 505-720-6593. I also have a personal website to blog about my thoughts about business brokerage and offer advice for both buyers and sellers, www.barbara-kline.com.

BARBARA KLINE, PH.D

Business Broker

Absolute Investment Realty, LLC

Barbara Kline, Ph.D., is a Certified Business Broker and a Senior Advisor with Absolute Investment Realty, a commercial real estate firm in Albuquerque, NM.

Barbara is a passionate supporter of business owners. She uses her experience to help business owners with property sales, purchases, and leases, as well as helping owners reap the rewards of their investment in their businesses at the time of sale. She was recently recognized as one of the top 25 business mentors in the United States in Alignable's Mainstreet Mentor search.

Barbara was a serial entrepreneur and real estate investor for many years prior to getting her certification as a business broker. She has founded numerous companies, including a public relations firm specializing in promoting technology startups in Silicon Valley, a day spa, an events center, and a publishing company. As a business mentor in the San Francisco Bay Area and a New Mexico Angel and TVC coach, she provided counsel on business strategy and funding proposals to startups throughout the Western United States. She has worked internationally, spending three years in Brussels with Intel and one year as VP of Global Marketing for a Dutch software company.

In her spare time, she travels widely, reads biographies and cozy mysteries, cooks, and is still attempting to learn how to grow vegetables in the New Mexico ecosystem.

EMAIL:
barbara@barbara-kline.com

PHONE:
505-720-6593

WEBSITE:
www.Barbara-Kline.com

OTHER:
www.go-Absolute.net

LINKEDIN:
linkedin.com/in/b-kline-business-broker

BOB DUNPHY

BOB DUNPHY

CONVERSATION WITH BOB DUNPHY

> ■ Bob, you are a business advisor with Transworld Business Advisors of New York. Tell us about your work and the people you help.

Bob Dunphy: In a word, I help small business owners sell their businesses and retire or reinvest in another enterprise. I personally target baby boomers looking to exit their businesses. It could be anything from a pizzeria in a downtown area or a strip mall to a chain of restaurants, optical stores, third-party logistics companies, retail stores, or a direct mail company; any business with sales up to about $30 million. It's a broad range of sizes; nothing is too small, almost nothing is too large. We are industry agnostic because we have worked with medical services, law firms, cell phone stores, restaurants, and manufacturing companies. If you own it, we can sell it.

LEADING BUSINESS INTERMEDIARIES, BROKERS, AND M&A ADVISORS

■ How informed are business owners about the selling process when they first meet with you?

Bob Dunphy: Most owners spend their lives *building* their businesses. They spend little or no time thinking about selling it. As a result, the entire process is new to them. Once they decide to sell, they may do some research, but, for most, it is the only time they will meet a business broker and go through the process. So it is critical to choose wisely and even more critical to follow your broker's guidance. They've done this many times before; you have not.

I was working with the owners of a business, and the sale included real estate. They took over the business from their father, so the store had been in the family for 70 years and in business for over 100 years. There were many challenges to navigate. They were great at running the retail side of the store but not as detailed about running the business side. They didn't even think about their exit until they decided to retire, which they wanted to do the following year. We can do that, but we can do a better job when a plan is in place.

There is a whole process of planning and preparing your business for sale, similar to selling a house. You might paint, fix up the kitchen, and update the bathroom. Some of it is cosmetic with a business, but you also need to get your legal and financial documents in order, make sure your staff is on their game and make your bottom line as strong as possible. You also want your business to be "transparent." When talking to a potential buyer, they need to see that what you say matches the financials, legalities, and liabilities exactly. That will help support the value and the price you are asking. It enhances the value.

Also, operationally, if you as the owner are the "go-to" person, it makes it harder to sell the business because you ARE the business. For example, if we have Marco's Italian Restaurant and Marco is there every night and stops at each table, the customers will always look for Marco. No Marco, less value. Some famous chefs like Daniel Boulud, Todd English, or Guy Fieri can get away with owning restaurants and not being there every night. But for the most part, if you are the "go-to" person - whether a tech, chef, baker, salesperson, or accountant - the person taking over the business risks losing some of your clients. If a doctor sells his medical practice and retires, will all of those patients stick around for the new doctor? It's important to make yourself *replaceable*.

■ How has the "Great Resignation" impacted your market?

Bob Dunphy: For employees, it's the "Great Resignation." For Baby Boomer business owners, it's the *"Silver Tsunami."* The peak years of the Baby Boom generation are turning 65. They were already thinking about retirement. Their experience over the last two years has pushed it front and center, and we expect many long-time business owners to hang out the "For Sale" sign. This sets up a huge generational shift in small business ownership as Millennials, Gen Xers, and Gen Ys take over.

If you have a good business, NOW is a great time to be *already selling* because you're ahead of the tsunami. There are plenty of good buyers in the market for solid businesses, and business valuations are strong. But, if more owners sell their businesses in the coming years, it could result in a Buyer's Market as supply outpaces demand. And that could mean less value for your business. It's all about supply and demand. If there's more supply and the same demand, those businesses will devalue because there are four of "you" for sale.

One of the benefits of the "Great Resignation" could be increased small business ownership. Not everyone wants to be a part of the "Gig Economy" or a solopreneur. Many will want a great business of their own, one with existing cash flow. That's a potential small business or franchise buyer.

■ How early should an owner start planning for the sale of their business?

Bob Dunphy: I was just having this conversation with someone. The short answer is: When you start the business. Look, the big venture capital firms want to know the exit strategy of a startup in the first pitch meeting. The question is: "If we give you all this money, how much will we make, and how soon will we get it?"

You have to know where you want to go in order to plan the journey. But another reason why it's always good to have an exit plan is that you never know - life happens. We've had people sell their business because of family health issues, partner disputes, relocations, or family abroad. We have people who started the business in their 20s and need to sell in their 30s instead of someone who is retiring. But if you're approaching retirement age, you should start cleaning up your act about five years before selling. Make sure your financials are in order, gather your legal documents, strengthen your team and make sure the business shows a solid, provable profit.

Suppose you haven't planned that far ahead; we can still sell your business. But it might not be as valuable as you thought, take longer to sell, or need more creative financing terms. I believe that just about any business can be sold if *everyone* involved is realistic about the value.

■ Bob, what inspired you to get started in this field?

Bob Dunphy: My original career was in the radio broadcasting business. I started on the creative side and eventually became a sales manager and a general manager. Most radio stations are small businesses, and I ran a couple of groups just outside New York City in northern New Jersey and the Hudson Valley. A publicly-traded company owned it, so I had to run a tight ship in terms of people and finances.

Part of my job was selling advertising to small business owners… the same folks I work with now. Then, my goal was to help them grow by marketing their business. I became friends with many through golf outings, charity boards, and other community events. I gained an understanding of small businesses and small business owners there. When a Radio friend of mine got into business brokerage, he suggested I join him. His pitch was simple: "You're already talking to these folks; now you can sell their businesses instead of pitching them advertising." I was kind of tired of commuting, frankly, so I changed careers.

Now the conversations are simpler; either you want to sell, or you don't. And if you want to sell, I can help you. Even though I'm not an exit planner, I can help with preparation, cleaning things up, and offering suggestions for improvement regarding marketing and resources. Perhaps we might bring in experts from different fields to help grow the business a little bit during the process because the average business takes about nine months to sell. Since I am with my clients for a while, we might as well do what we can to make things better during that time.

■ Is there anything else you would like to share?

Bob Dunphy: Right now, because of COVID-19, there are challenges with specific industries. There also are challenges in analyzing the recent history of any business. Most buyers want to look at three years of financials. If we look back, 2019 was probably the last solid year, 2020 was a mess, and 2021 should have been a recovery year, but the Omicron variant derailed even that. So how your business has been trending and how aggressively you managed to get back into it after the downturn is really important. For some industries, there's almost nothing these owners can do. I have a client in midtown Manhattan whose clients are all of the people in the office towers. But nobody is working inside of those towers just yet. They will be soon, but not today. He's just a victim of the "working from home" movement. In short, your trajectory, story, and coming out of the pandemic are critical.

■ How can people find you, connect with you, and learn more?

Bob Dunphy: Our website is www.tworld.com. If you add a slash and a Bob Dunphy to the end of that, you will find my page: www.tworld.com/bobdunphy. If you Google my name, I tend to come up near the top. My email is simply BDunphy@Tworld.com, and my phone is (917) 589-0977. I'm happy to speak with you about your business, no matter what stage you think you are at. I've worked with some of my clients, preparing them for three to four years before we listed them for sale to make sure they have the best possible outcome.

No part of this communication or its contents is intended to provide tax, financial or legal advice, and any statements referring to these areas are to be considered opinion only. All recipients are encouraged to take independent tax, financial or legal advice from duly regulated sources. Transworld Business Advisors and its agents provide a limited form of representation to a buyer, a seller, or both, that allows Transworld to facilitate a transaction but does not represent either in a fiduciary capacity or as a single agent.

BOB DUNPHY

Senior Business Broker & Franchise Consultant

Transworld Business Advisors of New York

Bob Dunphy is a veteran Business Broker and Franchise Consultant in the New York City office of Transworld Business Advisors. Bob works with business owners to match their businesses with the right buyers at the right price and terms. He also assists buyers with identifying the right business or franchise opportunity and aids with franchise development for owners of unique and scalable business concepts. Bob represents businesses in a wide variety of industries, including manufacturing, medical, restaurants & hospitality, retail, telecommunications, education, commercial real estate, and more. He works closely with his clients from valuation to presentation to letter of intent, financing, due diligence, and closing. He is a member of the Transworld President's Club.

Bob joined Transworld after a successful career as a media executive, where he specialized in startups, turnarounds, and team building. His experience ranges from business management and operations to sales and creative roles, and he has consulted a wide variety of businesses in sales, marketing, promotion, and advertising.

Whether you represent an acquisition-minded corporation or are personally interested in owning your own company, Transworld Business Advisors offers the professional services that successfully bring buyers and sellers together. From business brokerage to franchising to mergers and acquisitions, Transworld Business Advisors does Good Deals for Good People.

WEBSITE:
www.tworld.com/bobdunphy

PHONE:
917-589-0977

EMAIL:
BDunphy@Tworld.com

LINKEDIN:
https://www.linkedin.com/in/bobdunphy/

TWITTER:
https://twitter.com/Biz_Broker_Bob

INSTAGRAM:
https://www.instagram.com/bobdunphy/

FACEBOOK:
https://www.facebook.com/BizBrokerBob/

GOOGLE MY BUSINESS:
Transworld Business Advisors of New York Bob Dunphy

LAUREN DRUMMOND-DALE

LAUREN DRUMMOND-DALE

CONVERSATION WITH LAUREN DRUMMOND-DALE

■ **Lauren, you are the founder of Coastal Consultants LLC in Mississippi. Tell us about your work and the people you help.**

Lauren Drummond-Dale: In my area of the country, there aren't many business intermediaries, much fewer ones certified with the International Business Brokers Association. We're kind of a novelty. When business owners are ready to exit their businesses in this area, they don't know what to do. They think they either need to sell it to family or friends or close the doors. Our biggest challenge in South Mississippi, Louisiana, and Alabama is educating people that we exist and sell businesses all day, every day. Ideally, we would like to talk to business owners three or four years before they're ready to exit their business to make sure we have it positioned for the best return on their life's investment in that company.

When we speak with buyers, it is helpful for us to match them to the correct business if we know their financial capacity and comfort levels. We also consider what experiences in their career or life would help them operate a business.

▪ Are there myths and misconceptions about selling a business?

Lauren Drummond-Dale: We get stuck in a real trap when we try to tell people what we do. They say, "Oh, so you're like a realtor?" Well, no. I have a real estate license, and I'd be happy to sell your property if you own your property and your business. But your business transaction is much more complicated than a property transaction.

We help initiate, negotiate, and get the deal to the closing table for transactions in a highly confidential manner. Most business owners are experts at the business they operate but have had little or no experience buying or selling a business.

The ones who have done it on their own the first time come to us for the second one, and those who come to us for the first one, come back!

One huge myth is that finding a buyer is the key. We keep a database of buyers just waiting for the right business to come along, or if we have a committed buyer, we know how to reach out and find just the right business for them.

Another misconception in our practice is that the deal is done when we all leave the closing table. We believe that we become trusted business associates. In 99% of sales, the former owner stays available in some capacity to aid the new owner in the transition. We also stand by for any assistance we can provide. The largest portion of our business comes from repeat customers. An interesting thing about many entrepreneurs is their constant desire to challenge themselves, so once they master whatever business we sell them, they are ready to try a different one. And we are here to help them make that transition.

The sad situations are ones where there is illness or even a death forcing a sale. Every owner should be planning for their exit. The more preparation and planning there is, the less a tragedy will affect the company's value.

■ What pitfalls do you help business owners avoid when preparing for sale?

Lauren Drummond-Dale: Most small business owners operate their businesses with the least tax exposure they can legally have. The person buying the business is looking for the greatest cash flow after taxes. So those two numbers don't always coincide for the business owner's benefit. Sometimes entrepreneurs have great success at going out and selling things, but they're not the best bookkeepers. They need someone to clean their books up so that it's very clear what they're doing. Nothing should be a mystery to the buyer. Everything needs to be clear and concise. That's a lot of what we sometimes do up to a year before the owner takes the business to market. We clear up any mysteries that might be taking place in the books.

A couple of other things to remember are to keep running the business! Do not take your foot off of the accelerator, don't wait until you hit a downturn to sell.

Buyers don't handle surprises well during due diligence. We encourage our sellers to consider us confidants and tell us the good, the bad, and the ugly so that we best know how to clearly explain these things to a buyer.

▪ How has the "Great Resignation" impacted your market?

Lauren Drummond-Dale: It's a great time to buy or sell a business. There is money available to help people starting out who don't have a large amount of cash. The Small Business Administration still has its doors open; they still assist people in buying businesses. Business owners who are a little older have been through several sweeps of the economy, and many are not sure they want to ride another one out. Things are excellent now. We've been telling people for several years; now is the time to sell. Let's not wait for another slump when you don't have the greatest numbers in the world to show someone. Get your business ready. Even if it's not prepared this year, shoot for the first part of next year to get the greatest return on your lifetime investment.

■ **Lauren, what inspired you to get started in this field?**

Lauren Drummond-Dale: I've started and owned about a dozen different businesses in my career. Like most of my neighbors here in Mississippi, I didn't know there were business brokers to help sell smaller companies. We work with companies with up to $40 million in revenue, but we also help companies with $250,000 in revenue. So when I was exiting my companies for various reasons, I didn't know what to do. Now that I've had a little success in my life, I believe in reaching back and pulling the next entrepreneur up along with me. This is an excellent way for me to help business owners exit. Also, I get to help new business owners coming out of corporate America understand the differences between running a Main Street business versus being in the corporate world.

■ **Is there anything else you would like to share?**

Lauren Drummond-Dale: The number one concern of business owners is confidentiality. That is the key difference between using a business intermediary or M&A (mergers and acquisitions) advisor versus a realtor. A realtor puts your business or property on MLS for everyone to see. We work entirely confidentially through our marketing, preparing, and negotiating. We get you to the closing without everyone on the street, including your vendors and customers, finding out it is for sale until a deal is firmly on the table.

Feel confident that we do not pressure our clients. We stand ready to help you gather the facts you need to make a decision and discuss ways to make and adjust an exit strategy, all while maintaining confidentiality. We are here to support, educate, and guide you when you are ready.

Having owned and operated businesses ourselves, we appreciate the magnitude of a transition of ownership.

■ How can people find you, connect with you, and learn more?

Lauren Drummond-Dale: The name of my company is Coastal Consultants LLC in Mississippi. We are on LinkedIn, and our website is www.coastalconsult.org. We would be glad to talk to anyone and never charge for an initial conversation, whether you are a buyer or a seller, to see if we can help before we get down to business. We're not hard sell. We consider ourselves intermediaries, and we're trying to find common ground between an owner who wants to exit and a buyer who wants to enter the business.

LAUREN DRUMMOND-DALE, CBI, M&A ADVISOR

Founder

Coastal Consultants LLC

Lauren Drummond-Dale is a CBI (Certified Business Intermediary) for Coastal Consultants LLC, a Business Brokerage and M&A Firm that handles Business Valuations, Sales, Mergers and Acquisition Advisory Services. She is also a Commercial Realtor with Marcellus Realty Inc. and a past director of Business Networking International.

She is a former SCORE Counselor and veteran business owner of 30-plus years for over a dozen companies.

Lauren has owned, operated, and managed multiple businesses in the areas of retail, construction, disaster relief, property development, demolition, oil exploration, forestry products, and pipeline remediation.

Her experience includes developing a business organization and management team that allowed several businesses to quickly grow from 5 employees and $200,000 in annual sales to over 200 employees and in excess of $15 million in sales. She has developed business plans for companies reaching for $500,000 in annual revenues and those planning on >$250 million in annual revenues.

As a Business Broker, Consultant and Realtor, she can focus her expertise, experience, and knowledge of business operations and challenges to benefit other entrepreneurs who want to grow their business, start a business or even retire from business.

Lauren has made the MS Gulf Coast her home and enjoys networking activities, triathlons, kayaking, bicycling, and most of all, her two sons and granddaughters.

EMAIL:
Lauren@coastalconsult.org

PHONE:
Office:+1.228.424.1024 Cell:
601.917.8496

WEBSITE:
www.coastalconsult.org

LINKEDIN:
https://www.linkedin.com/in/laurendrummond/

FACEBOOK:
https://www.facebook.com/search/top?q=coastal%20consultants

INSTAGRAM:
https://www.instagram.com/coastal_consultants/

KEVIN A. NERY

KEVIN A. NERY

CONVERSATION WITH KEVIN A. NERY

■ **Kevin, you are the Founder of Coastal M&A. Tell us about your work and the people you help.**

Kevin A. Nery: I've been at this for 22 years now. We have a small boutique Merger and Acquisition (M&A) firm in Massachusetts. Because of our location, we focus on manufacturing, wholesale distribution, service companies, construction trades, and hospitality. Over the years, we have helped owners in many different industries sell their businesses or companies. I am a Lifetime Certified Business Intermediary (LCBI), and a Merger and Acquisitions Master Intermediary (M&AMI).

■ **Are owners typically well-prepared to sell their businesses?**

Kevin A. Nery: Some are well prepared, but the typical scenario is an owner who started the business on a smaller budget, bootstrapping it over the years, growing it, and becoming successful. They usually don't start out planning to sell their business. But a good recommendation for folks establishing a business is always thinking in terms of the future. It helps you to grow and become more professional. I see many owners who are too caught up in the day-to-day aspect of business and don't have a vision or strategy for their exit or retirement.

■ What common concerns do owners have when preparing to sell?

Kevin A. Nery: Confidentiality is always a concern. Owners don't want anyone to know they are putting the business up for sale and feel awkward about it. If word gets out in the business community, it could be troublesome. They often have long-term relationships with employees and key staff members, so it is stressful to think about having those conversations. Though it is a confidential process, sometimes we will have the owner tap into one or two key employees to let them know their plans for the future, especially if they will need information from them during the sale process or if those employees would stay on to help the new owner run the business beyond the transition.

■ Are there any myths or misconceptions about selling a business?

Kevin A. Nery: The guy at the country club always tells everyone he sold his business for $20 million or some other exaggerated number. So "fake news" or misinformation can be a problem when it comes to having realistic expectations for the value of your business. Nobody will simply plunk down a pile of money at the closing table. The reality is that there are all different deal structures. I just came out of a meeting with two brothers who have grown their company tremendously. They are in the construction trade and have an offer, but it wasn't exactly the offer they thought it was initially. Working capital, consulting agreements, and tax issues must be accounted for. So somebody can't just give you a number. There are many tiny components of a deal structure.

■ Kevin, what inspired you to get started in this field?

Kevin A. Nery: My background is very interesting. Right out of college, I worked for Shawmut Bank, one of the largest banks in Boston, in the Custodial Accounting Department. I was responsible for four mutual funds for a "small" company called Fidelity in the 70s when they were just starting out. From there, I worked for public accounting firms and in manufacturing and ultimately owned my own business, which my wife and I sold 22 years ago. By that time, I had all the skills and experience to go out and become an intermediary.

■ Is there anything else you would like to share?

Kevin A. Nery: If you consider selling your business, seek a trusted advisor. Even though there is a lot of information out there in the form of the internet and books, you really need someone to help navigate the process, maintain confidentiality, make negotiations, handle marketing, and negotiate. Not to mention, you need someone who can determine the proper value for your business. Many owners tend to think the business is worth a bit more than what it actually is. So an advisor with experience is vital. We have sold over 250 businesses in 22 years. Every opportunity is unique and requires someone with skills and knowledge to represent the client well.

■ How can people find you, connect with you, and learn more?

Kevin A. Nery: It's very easy. My phone number is 508-990-9800. You can email me at k.nery@nerycorp.com. My website is www.coastalmanda.com. We have a wealth of information on that site. Give me a call anytime, and I'd be happy to have a discussion and answer any questions you may have.

KEVIN A. NERY, CBB, LCBI, M&AMI

President, Certified Business Intermediary,
M&A Master Intermediary

Coastal M&A

Kevin A. Nery, CBB, LCBI, M&AMI, President, has over 40 years of business experience in the areas of accounting, taxation, management, manufacturing, marketing, and consulting. He has achieved the Certified Business Broker (CBB), Lifetime Certified Business Intermediary (LCBI), Merger and Acquisitions Master Intermediary (M&AMI), Business Transfer Specialist (BTS), and Financial Recasting Consultant (FRC) professional designations. Mr. Nery is a Graduate of Fairleigh Dickinson University with a Bachelor's Degree in Accounting. As a professional business intermediary, Mr. Nery is able to utilize his personal and professional experiences in start-ups, buying, selling, and owning his own companies. He has held positions in banking, manufacturing, CPA firms, and a retail corporation before founding the firm in 2000. Over the years, Mr. Nery has sold over 250 businesses and companies and valued hundreds of businesses, professional firms, and companies. He has extensive knowledge of business sales, mergers, acquisitions, business valuations, and commercial real estate sales and leasing.

Mr. Nery is affiliated nationally with The International Business Brokers Association (IBBA) and The M & A Source. He currently serves on the Board of Directors of the New England Business Brokers Association (NEBBA) as Treasurer.

Mr. Nery is also a Member of the New Bedford Economic Development Council, the One SouthCoast Chamber of Commerce, and was a Featured Columnist in the monthly "South Coast Business Bulletin" for many years. He has been a Guest Speaker on WBSM 1420 AM's weekly show, "Money Wise," and a Contributing Intermediary with BIZCOMPS© Completed Business Sales Statistics. He was also named to the Hall of Fame for Pratt's Stats® Sold Business Database.

EMAIL:
K.Nery@nerycorp.com

PHONE:
508-990-9800

WEBSITE:
www.CoastalMandA.com

LINKEDIN:
https://www.linkedin.com/company/coastalmanda

KELLY M. HAYES

KELLY M. HAYES

CONVERSATION WITH KELLY M. HAYES

■ **Kelly, you are the Co-founder of Siegel, Greenfield & Hayes PLC. Tell us about your work and the people you help.**

Kelly M. Hayes: I'm an attorney, CPA, and licensed real estate broker. My focus is on representing the buyer or the seller of a business. Often, the seller is trying to transfer the business successfully to the next generation of children or relatives. I work with businesses in the $1 million to $20 million range, including staffing firms, salons, manufacturers, child care centers, accounting firms, and retail stores. Because of my background, I'm able to look at the financials, give the seller an idea of possible value, look at the bank financing, and assist them with papering the transaction.

■ Are sellers well-prepared for selling their businesses?

Kelly M. Hayes: Most of them are not prepared because their decisions are a little more spontaneous than they should be. To be a good seller, you need to start prepping a year and a half to two years before the sale. Financials need to be in order, and documentation needs to be in place so that you can make a coherent and accurate presentation to potential buyers.

■ Are there myths and misconceptions about selling a business?

Kelly M. Hayes: One of the biggest problems I face is that when someone throws out a value to a seller (a lot of times, it is coming from an accountant or an insurance agent), they will give an off-the-cuff remark like, "Oh, you can sell your business for $3 million." Suddenly, the seller is stuck on that number. When we actually do the valuation of the business or when a savvy buyer comes in to do a valuation, the seller finds out that $3 million is just way too high. So as an advisor to the seller, it can be difficult for me to get them "unstuck" from that number. In addition, many sellers don't realize how their financial statements look. Savvy buyers will point out things that don't make sense financially and walk away from a potential sale or start a negotiation process to reduce the price.

■ How have the pandemic and the "Great Resignation" impacted your market?

Kelly M. Hayes: The problem that sellers face right now is that they probably all had a down year in 2020 because of the pandemic. In 2021, many of them rebounded, but if you're a buyer looking at three years of averages, 2020 creates some negatives for the seller. With respect to the Great Resignation, I have seen many executives leaving corporate America wanting to start or buy their own businesses. A lot of them are looking at franchises.

■ Kelly, what inspired you to get started in this field?

Kelly M. Hayes: I started in public accounting and then went to law school at night. I started with my first law firm in 1988. I was more focused on estate planning and other tax-type issues. But with any sale or purchase of a business, you always have tax issues. So that's a background theme that runs through all of these transactions. Also, with the sale of a business, if you're representing the seller, you have estate planning issues because these sellers are coming into a large chunk of money, so you have to do tax planning, and you have to do estate planning for them. It was a natural progression for me. I had a friend who introduced me to the Michigan Business Brokers Association, a member of the IBBA. I joined and started attending their meetings, where I met a lot of different business brokers. They were all great at the sales part of it and at finding potential buyers, but their forte is not necessarily advising the seller or buyer on how to structure a transaction.

■ What should owners focus on to make their businesses attractive and sellable?

Kelly M. Hayes: I advise owners to look at their equipment and make sure it is up to date and in good working order. Look at the real estate for any potential problems or environmental issues. Overall, ensure the facility is in excellent shape.

I also see many situations where some of the business was done in cash, and that cash may not be hitting the financial statements. The seller knows it's there, but the buyer and the bank don't. And they need proof of earnings. By not having the most accurate books, a seller may end up discounting the value of their business.

■ Is there anything else you would like to share?

Kelly M. Hayes: If you are considering buying a business, you need to do your due diligence, especially if you are unfamiliar with the field. Bring in a team of people who can help you with the areas you don't know. A banker can help familiarize you with SBA or conventional financing. You also want to consult an insurance professional, a CPA, and a good attorney. Let them do what they specialize in while you, as the buyer, can focus on the actual operation of the business and what's there and not there.

■ **How can people find you, connect with you, and learn more?**

Kelly M. Hayes: You can email me at khayes@sghplc.com. I can also be reached by phone at 248-386-5900. I talk to people all the time, and I don't charge them for a call to establish a relationship and see how I can help. We don't have a website, as most of our business comes from referrals from bankers, CPAs, insurance professionals, existing clients, and brokers.

KELLY M. HAYES, J.D., C.P.A.

Co-Founder

Siegel, Greenfield & Hayes PLC

Kelly M. Hayes was born in Bay City, Michigan. He was admitted to the Michigan Bar in 1988. Kelly attended the University of Detroit (B.S.B.A., magna cum laude, 1981) and Wayne State University (J.D., 1988, AmJur award in Taxation). He is a Certified Public Accountant-Michigan (Registered, not Licensed) and a member of the State Bar of Michigan, Alabama State Bar, American Institute of Certified Public Accountants, and Michigan Association of Certified Public Accountants. Kelly is a Founder and owner of the law firm Siegel, Greenfield & Hayes P.L.C., located in Southfield, Michigan. He specializes in representing buyers and sellers of businesses, providing tax advice, succession planning, and estate and asset protection planning. Kelly has been practicing law for 34 years; he's been a CPA for over 39 years.

EMAIL:
khayes@sghplc.com

PHONE:
248-386-5900 x515

VIRGINIA ALTMAN

VIRGINIA ALTMAN

CONVERSATION WITH VIRGINIA ALTMAN

> ■ **Virginia, you are the Founder and CEO of The Exit Eagle. Tell us about your work and the people you help.**

Virginia Altman: I'll preface it by telling you how I got into it. I ended up owning my family's business and discovered three years into it that the nephew who was preparing to take it over was serious when he said he didn't want it. So that started me on a journey of learning how to sell businesses. That was in 2006, and since then, I have been encouraged to found a company to help business owners in the small to mid-sized markets. I love working with business owners who have never been exposed to this process because I educate them along the way. Money counts, but what *really* matters is how the owner feels when they reach the end of the process. So most of my clients are small to mid-sized business owners who have not bought or sold many businesses.

■ What concerns do business owners have regarding selling?

Virginia Altman: They are mostly wondering, "How do I do this?" That sounds very generic, but most of them don't even know where to start. That's exactly how I felt when I was faced with this situation. So the first time we meet, I simply go over the process and explain it from beginning to end. I show them their business valuation, which is always a mystery. We will also go over the sale prospectus, the primary vehicle for communicating why somebody should buy the business. I generate support documents from financials, and at the end, we do what I call a "sweat test" to see if the business is ready to be sold. It has been designed over the past 15 years to make owners sweat a little and give them the opportunity to correct some things to increase value.

■ Are there myths and misconceptions about selling a business?

Virginia Altman: People think if you put it on the market, it will sell. But 80% of businesses on the market *don't* sell. The other interesting fact is that only one-third of buyers find a business to buy. So that really reveals a lot about just putting it on the market and expecting it to sell.

The other myth is that you can get whatever you want from your business. Owners think all of their sweat equity will be returned. But it just doesn't happen that way.

■ What are common mistakes owners make to sabotage the sale of their business?

Virginia Altman: The number one mistake they make is not having their financials ready to be examined closely. The buyer needs to see whether or not they will make money from it. The worst example I can give is a mechanic who owned a garage. He wrote all the appointments by hand in his calendar and jotted the names and phone numbers, but you could not read the majority of them, and we could not come up with a customer list, nor could we come up with any viable financials. Don't even leave the mark if you don't have those two things.

■ How soon should owners start preparing for the sale of their business?

Virginia Altman: Theoretically, you should start the day you open your business. Whatever targets you set are the ones you are most likely to meet. The target should be increasing, and you should be paying attention to value to sell it well. But rarely does somebody who's just starting a business have the mental capacity to begin to add on. So another thought is three years before the sale because buyers look at three to five years worth of financials and other documents in the business. So if you don't have your financials right and the matching tax returns for at least three years, it will probably hinder selling or getting a good price.

> ■ **Virginia, what inspired you to get started in this field?**

Virginia Altman: There are two factors. Before owning the family business, I was a change management and turnaround consultant in the Fortune 500 environment. In that capacity, I often worked with Goldman Sachs, which would generate the valuation, and my job was to increase that value. So we would meet quarterly to review the valuation and see what improvements had been made. I loved helping to increase value. And that is the first thing I did in my family's business. So that's part one.

Then when I realized I had to sell my family business, I just sat there like, "How do I sell it?" I knew it could be done and that I could put a price on it, but I didn't know exactly how the process worked. I tried to get help from my attorney and accountant, but they just sent me to somebody else. Nobody was willing to help me. So I ended up in Pittsburgh at an investment banker's office. They asked if I had $30 million in revenue. And honestly, that was a joke. No way did I have $30 million in revenue. So they wouldn't help me either. It was all up to me. That began my crusade to learn how to do it and help others do it instead of going back to the big Fortune 500 world.

- **How can people find you, connect with you, and learn more?**

Virginia Altman: The website for my business is www.theexiteagle.com. You can also phone or text me at 412-514-1050.

VIRGINIA ALTMAN, MPM, CBI, CEPA

Founder and CEO

The Exit Eagle

The Exit Eagle's mission is to help business owners to prepare to exit their businesses in a way that attracts Next Generation owners. The seed for starting the business developed in 2006 and 2007 as Virginia Altman, founder and CEO, was selling her family's business

– a completely unexpected event that took place after accepting that the Third Generation did not want the 24/7 responsibility of the business.

Prior to becoming Second Generation owner of her family's telecommunications business, Virginia was a turnaround/ change management consultant for 20 years in the Fortune 500 environment. Her two favorite projects were implementing Total Quality Management into Ford Electronics Division, where she collapsed the Electronics Division's product development timeline from 180 to 36 months; and, as a consultant to Corning Consumer Products Division, turned a -6% ROI into a +14% ROI over a two-year period – which increased the sale price from $350 million to $700+ million.

After working in seven countries, Virginia moved back to the Greensburg area to be near her parents. She became the owner of their family business in 2004 and sold it in 2007. She started Altman Business Solutions, LLC (dba The Exit Eagle) in 2008 and has since helped more than 40 business owners to exit their businesses.

Virginia earned her Master's in Public Management (with an emphasis on Investment Banking) from Carnegie Mellon University and her undergraduate degree from Seton Hill University. She is a Certified Exit Planning Advisor (CEPA), Certified Business Intermediary (CBI) and has numerous certifications in change management processes, facilitation, and thinking tools.

EMAIL:
Virginia.Altman@TheExitEagle.com

PHONE:
412.514.1050

WEBSITE:
www.TheExitEagle.com

LINKEDIN:
https://www.linkedin.com/in/virginiaaltman

"JT" JIM TATEM

"JT" JIM TATEM

CONVERSATION WITH "JT" JIM TATEM

> ■ **JT, you are a business advisor with Transworld Business Advisors of Greenville, South Carolina. Tell us about your work and the people you help.**

"JT" Jim Tatem: At Transworld, we do three things as good or better than anyone else. Our first expertise is business brokerage, advising owners looking to transition and sell their businesses. Perhaps it is time for them to retire, spend more time with their family, or buy an island in the Caribbean. Whatever their motivation, we work with them to establish the right selling price, bring the business to the market, find the right buyer, and bring them both together to make their successful transaction happen.

Second, some business owners we work with aren't interested in selling. They say, "JT, my business is doing so great. I wish I had ten of them." In that case, we help them turn their concept into a franchise business through Accurate Franchising, one of our sister companies. I've been in the franchising space for nearly 35 years, and I know it very well.

Third, we work with buyers interested in one of our independent businesses, and maybe that type of business is right for them. Sometimes it's not. If they are first-time business owners, they often need training, marketing, support, and branding. These are all things they can benefit from by owning a franchise. So, in addition to dozens of existing businesses we offer for sale, we also present over 400 different franchise concepts to match buyers with and find the ideal opportunity for each one.

■ How knowledgeable are business owners about the selling process?

"JT" Jim Tatem: That's a great question. We work with a broad spectrum from Main Street Mom and Pop pizza shops, nail salons, and auto repair shops, all the way up to the middle market and M&A world, with businesses generating $5 million to $10 million a year in revenue. This first group tends to have spent all of their time, effort, and energy building the business, leaving very little time to think about an exit strategy and how to sell their business. So, they need a lot of coaching and hand-holding throughout the process. They are on a journey to take what they have built and get a good return on investment, but they don't know the steps of the process. We stay alongside them and help get them to the finish line. When you go to the middle market space and the M&A world, those tend to be more sophisticated sellers. They often have a team of people working with them on the accounting and legal sides, and they have great books and records. They have balance sheets, and their systems and processes are very well documented. They tend to be more prepared to sell and have actually thought about an exit strategy. Since we have seen both ends of the spectrum, we're equipped to help clients on either end and everywhere in between.

> ■ **Statistics show that 80% of businesses on the market never sell. What are some of the most common reasons for this?**

"JT" Jim Tatem: It's an interesting statistic. At Transworld, we have a higher percentage of businesses that list and actually sell. Part of that is our preparation to get the business ready to bring to the market. Just because you want to sell something doesn't mean it is sellable. It would be similar to having a dilapidated house that needs a new paint job and window replacements. You have to fix those items before you try to sell to increase curb appeal. And if you want to sell your car, you better wash it first. If you're going to sell your business, good books and records are the first things a potential buyer will look for. Make sure your accounting is being done correctly. Certain businesses are heavily credit card/purchase order oriented, so most sales are recorded easily. But there are other businesses with a large percentage of cash, which needs to come through to the tax return and profit and loss statement. Every dollar you bring in that winds up as profit gets a multiple applied to it for the business's selling price. The more profit you show, the higher your selling price will likely be.

Also, you'll want to focus on curb appeal. I always say to my sellers, "If you or your wife walked through this business for the first time, what things would you see that excite you? What things would turn you off? Let's fix the turn-offs." I've been married for 38 years now, and if my wife and I go to a restaurant and the bathroom isn't clean, we're out of there. She thinks, "If they can't keep the bathroom clean, what does the kitchen look like?"

In addition, do you have a good lease in place? If you are leasing the space, you don't want to get to the point where you are on a month-to-month basis and not sure whether or not you want to re-sign. That doesn't give a lot of security to the new buyer coming in. Ensuring that you have an excellent location locked down with a good lease negotiated is important.

Then there's your industry. Industry appeal plays a role as well. It should be a staple business instead of an "overnight sensation" that nobody has ever heard of. When you're gone, the buyer wants to be reassured there is still a need for the business in the local marketplace.

You'll also want processes in place. Documented and easy to follow. That makes your business worth more to your buyer. They'll want to know they can replicate your processes and systems to keep the customers satisfied. So, get everything you and your team know down on paper.

And that team we just mentioned is important too. If the business is wrapped up in just you, and everything revolves around you at the center, that could concern your buyer. They may think there's too much risk that the sales and clients will leave when you leave. So duplicate yourself. Replace yourself. Make it easy for a new owner to come in and not miss a beat.

■ How has the "Great Resignation" impacted your market?

"JT" Jim Tatem: It's a unique time for buying and selling businesses. The last several years have been very seller-focused. Now the baby boomers are leaving as they are ready to retire, and a new generation is coming in who don't want to work for the same company for 20 to 30 years and get a gold watch like grandpa did. They want to be the next Elon Musk or Mark Zuckerberg, controlling their own destinies. Owning a business is a great way to do that. Relatively speaking, financing is still pretty easy to come by. Money is fairly cheap until we see what happens next. All of that makes for very interesting demographics both coming in and exiting the market simultaneously. It's been a boom for us. Many people call us week after week, saying, "I'm ready. How do I get my business prepared?" On the other side, the people laid off or furloughed due to COVID decided they didn't want someone else in control of their future anymore, which drove them towards business ownership.

■ JT, what inspired you to get started in this field?

"JT" Jim Tatem: As I mentioned earlier, I've been in franchising for more than 30+ years. I started in a small sign and graphics business on Long Island, New York, in 1986 called Speedy Signarama USA. Eventually, Signarama became a franchise about a year and a half later. I was fortunate enough to start in the very first store. The owner of the company sold the signs, and I made the signs. That's how we began. We then franchised the business growing to over 700 locations in 60 countries worldwide. So I've been in the franchising space for a long time, helping people get into business, grow the business, and sell the business eventually. And as that brand Signarama continued to grow, we added new franchise concepts to the family. About 12 years ago, Transworld was a local business brokerage firm in Fort Lauderdale, Florida. And our franchise business was located an hour north in West Palm Beach. They were looking to expand outside of the state of Florida and thought franchising would be a good mechanism to do that. At the same time, our franchise company had about half a dozen different brands. We were looking to get into business brokerage to help franchise owners who were looking to exit their franchise find the right buyer. It really was a marriage made in Heaven. Transworld Business Advisors was born from Transworld Business Brokers and the folks at United Franchise Group.

At the time, I was the President of the Signarama concept and, for about four years, the President of United Franchise Group as a whole. I was watching these new franchise brands come aboard. I was fascinated by all the different industries that we got involved with. However, because of our international footprint, I was also gone a lot of the time. When you have 1,600 franchises in 80 countries worldwide, you don't spend much time at home. I know I can't get that time back, and I made a choice to do that type of work at the time. I also know a lot of folks who wish they did their careers differently. So after 30 years, I went to Ray Titus, the CEO, and owner of United Franchise Group. He's the guy that started selling the signs in that first store back in 1986. We've worked together a long time and can be kind of like an old married couple. He nagged me at times, and I finished his sentences. But it's been a tremendously rewarding relationship. I said, "This has been great. I have loved what we have done. I have amazing relationships all over the world. But quite frankly, I've taught other people how to get into business and be successful for over 30 years. And I'd like to take my own shot." He said, "Tell me what you want to do, JT, and I will help you get there."

So we decided that the best thing was a relocation for my family and me. We moved from West Palm Beach, Florida, to Greenville, South Carolina. We opened our office in Greenville, SC, and another in Asheville, NC. The biggest benefit is being with my wife every day and seeing my kids, who are now having kids. We have seven grandkids, one just born earlier this week, as a matter of fact. I get to sleep in my own bed every night, which was something I didn't do for 30+ years. I get to be part of the local fabric of our communities. And I get to be an active part of my family's lives- picnics, hikes, ball games, and field trips. Those are legacy moves in my mind - making memories my family will cherish. So that was my motivation - to go into business for myself as part of the Transworld Network and be able to help people buy into a business, grow a business, or sell a business, and do all of that on a local level and become the trusted local advisor.

It's very similar to the many stories I hear from our clients looking to buy a business week after week. You may have been an executive, or an employee, working for someone else for a long time and want the benefit of working for yourself. You're not afraid of doing the hard work. You just figure, if you're going to work that hard, you ought to gain the rewards. Or perhaps you've built a business of your own. You're ready to retire. Or maybe switch paths and do something completely different, so you need to find the best way to capitalize on your efforts and get a good return on your investment. Finding a good buyer to take over and grow what you've started can be a great option. Maybe you want to sell it to your staff. Or structure a deal with your family taking over. Or just completely cash out and move on. You can get the help you need to make any of those dreams come true.

- **How can people find you, connect with you, and learn more?**

"JT" Jim Tatem: There are three quick and easy ways. The first is to call my mobile and my office line. They're one and the same: 864-315-8998. You can also email me at jt1@tworld.com. Or scan the QR code and connect to my digital card and contact.

"JT" JIM TATEM

President and Lead Advisor

Transworld Business Advisors of Greenville, South Carolina & Asheville WNC

Since 1986, "JT" Jim Tatem has assisted over 3000 entrepreneurs in buying, growing, and selling their businesses. His career in franchising was launched in 1986, opening Signarama's first store in NY, building a brand that is currently over 700 locations in 60 countries worldwide. That first franchise led to 10 future brands and his role as President of the franchise parent company. For over 33 years, he's been guiding business owners on sales, growth, strategic planning, financial review, exit planning, and business development. He is experienced in international business, leading teams, business sales, support, sourcing, business finance, conventions, and events; his expertise is focused on driving your success as a business owner. JT leads the local Upstate SC and Asheville/WNC Transworld Business Advisors teams helping you capitalize on the benefits of business ownership. He's a licensed real estate agent in SC and NC, a CFE (Certified Franchise Executive), Vice President of Transworld Business Advisors Ad Fund Board, CVBBA Board Member, and active in his local church, Rotary, and Chambers of Commerce. Father of 4, Grandfather to 7, and Husband for 38 years, his mantra is to "Leave people better than I found them." When you need personable, persistent professionalism, put JT and the team to work for you.

EMAIL:
jt1@tworld.com

PHONE:
864-315-8998

WEBSITE:
www.tworld.com/UpstateSC
www.tworld.com/AshevilleWNC

LINKEDIN:
https://www.linkedin.com/in/jttatem/

FACEBOOK:
@TworldUpstateSC

MICHAEL D. MAUGER

MICHAEL D. MAUGER

CONVERSATION WITH MICHAEL D. MAUGER

■ **Michael, you are an Associate Broker with McGrath Business Group in Tampa, Florida. Tell us about your work and the people you help.**

Michael D. Mauger: I am a business broker and a commercial real estate broker; those two go hand in hand. Specifically, I work with clients who want to sell their businesses and people looking to purchase businesses. Many people are migrating from the Northeast down to Florida, so that market segment is growing rapidly.

■ **How prepared are business owners when it comes time to sell?**

Michael D. Mauger: It ranges from very prepared to unprepared. The most important thing an owner needs to do to prepare is to understand what their business is worth by discussing it with someone like their accountant or me. They should also have very strong financial statements so that we can clearly explain the business to a prospective buyer, ensuring they understand how the business works.

▪ Are there myths and misconceptions about selling a business?

Michael D. Mauger: Owners typically think their business is worth a lot more than it actually is. The market determines the price, not the seller. The selling price is typically a function of the profitability or owner benefit of the business. The market values the business based on that figure.

▪ A statistic states, "80% of businesses that go to market don't sell." What are some reasons for this?

Michael D. Mauger: The first would be a lack of clarity in the financial situation. Many businesses don't have good books and records. Secondly, some business owners have unrealistic expectations about what they can achieve regarding sale price. As mentioned previously, most owners value their businesses much higher than what a proper valuation would indicate.

■ How should owners prepare for the sale of their business?

Michael D. Mauger: The most important thing is to consult a qualified business broker to give them an understanding of what the process is. The first step would be to put a value on the business. That requires some accounting exercises to define the owner benefit. Then we talk about how to market the business. Some people want to keep it confidential. Therefore, the broker has a little more difficulty placing the ads on the internet because they don't want it to be known. The process typically takes between six and nine months to get to the closing table. But there are several steps in defining what's being sold, what's included in the sale, whether or not the employees will continue to stay, whether inventory is included, whether accounts receivable are included, and whether or not they are willing to sign a non-compete. Many people won't want to buy a business if the seller plans to open up a shop right down the street. So many of those things are factored in and typically covered through negotiation.

■ What type and size of businesses have you sold?

Michael D. Mauger: I work with purchase prices between 100k and 10 million dollars, with my sweet spot being between 1 and 5 million dollars. I have worked with buyers and sellers of all different kinds of businesses. Some examples include software, Assisted Living Facilities (ALFs), restaurants, gas stations, convenience stores, pest control, aquaculture, and automotive repair. Even coin laundromats and car washes!

■ As we are coming out of a pandemic, is this a good time to buy and sell businesses?

Michael D. Mauger: The market here in Tampa is extremely hot. Many people are moving to the area. People relocating from the Northeast or colder places like Chicago are coming to Florida and bringing significant amounts of money to set up their own businesses. I also get a lot of people from out of the country looking to "buy their way in" through a visa and the purchase of a business. There are programs available for foreigners to earn citizenship through business ownership.

■ Michael, what inspired you to get started in this field?

Michael D. Mauger: I was working in corporate America and was in the process of helping to buy and sell the division in which I worked. Through that process, I kind of got the deal fever. And based on that, and being impacted by rightsizing, downsizing, and outsourcing, I wanted to do something where I could control my own destiny. Therefore, I moved to Florida from the Northeast, desiring to help people sell businesses and buy businesses to achieve their financial dreams. Now I work with McGrath Business Group, have control over my daily activities, and enjoy working with other entrepreneurs to fulfill their dreams.

■ Is there anything else you would like to share?

Michael D. Mauger: People need to understand that selling a business is not easy. It typically takes six to nine months. It's not like selling a car or a house. It's a process. There is a lot of relationship-building that needs to go on between a buyer and a seller, and there needs to be a good feeling and a good fit so they can get to the closing table, both feeling like they are achieving a win.

■ How can people find you, connect with you, and learn more?

Michael D. Mauger: You can Google my name. My website is www.doylemcgrath.com. I'm also on many websites containing my listings, including ww.bizbuysell.com and www.bbf.com. That's the Business Brokers of Florida, where I have my portfolio of businesses for sale. Lastly, my email address is Mike@doylemcgrath.com.

MICHAEL D. MAUGER

Associate Broker

McGrath Business Group

Michael (Mike) Mauger is a business broker helping buyers and sellers to buy and sell businesses as well as the underlying commercial real estate. Mike is licensed in the state of Florida but conducts most of his business in the Tampa area, his city of residence. Mike has an MBA from Vanderbilt University and a Bachelor of Science in Business from the University of Connecticut. Mike is currently a Broker Associate at McGrath Business Group, a regional firm, but has also worked at national firms such as GMAC, Prudential, and Berkshire Hathaway.

Mike has had tremendous success in closing deals. Since 2004, Mike has closed over $100 million in transactions. To get to the closing table, Mike helps his clients place a value on the business, negotiate favorable terms, assist in due diligence, conduct buyer/seller relationship-building meetings, and secure financing. He has extensive relationships with local and regional banks and private finance companies.

Mike's ideal client is someone looking to buy or sell a business (or real estate) in the one to five million dollar range.

EMAIL:
mdmauger@gmail.com

PHONE:
813.995.3864

WEBSITE:
www.doylemcgrath.com

ABOUT THE PUBLISHER

Mark Imperial is a Best-Selling Author, Syndicated Business Columnist, Syndicated Radio Host, and internationally recognized Stage, Screen, and Radio Host of numerous business shows spotlighting leading experts, entrepreneurs, and business celebrities.

His passion is to discover noteworthy business owners, professionals, experts, and leaders who do great work and share their stories and secrets to their success with the world on his syndicated radio program titled "Remarkable Radio."

Mark is also the media marketing strategist and voice for some of the world's most famous brands. You can hear his voice over the airwaves weekly on Chicago radio and worldwide on iHeart Radio.

Mark is a Karate black belt; teaches Muay Thai and Kickboxing; loves Thai food, House Music, and his favorite TV shows are infomercials.

Learn more:

www.MarkImperial.com
www.BooksGrowBusiness.com

Made in the USA
Middletown, DE
11 July 2022